The Time Of Angels Is At Hand

Inspired Writings
By
Sandra J Yearman

Seraphim Publishing LLC

WE WILL BRING LIGHT TO ALL THE DARK PLACES

Registered trademark-Sandra J Yearman
Seraphim Publishing
438 Water St
Cambridge, WI 53523

Copyright © 2008 Sandra J Yearman
Produced in the United States of America
Author: Sandra J Yearman
Editor: Sandra J Yearman
Cover Design by Sandra J Yearman
Layout and design by Sandra J Yearman

All rights reserved. No part of this book may be reproduced, stored in or introduced into a retrieval system, or transmitted, in any form or by any means, electronic or mechanical, including photocopying or recording or otherwise copied for public or private use—other than for "fair use" as brief quotations embodied in articles and reviews--without written permission from the author.

Library of Congress Control Number: 2009900969
ISBN: 978-0-9815791-1-5
First Edition

We Should Be Singing Love Songs
For The Angels Heaven Sent
For The Wonder Of Life
For Love As It Was Meant
Amen
Amen
Amen

CONTENTS

DEDICATION

The Time Of Angels Is At Hand.......................7
The Angels Sing With Glory............................9
Holding Hands With Jesus.............................12
A Love Song..15
Divinity 17
Faith..19
The Living Flames Of Heaven 21
Jesus Is The Song...24
Wonderment...27
Abundance..29
Bless Us With Your Presence 30
A Little Angel 32
The White Bird Of Christmas........................34
Blood And The Crown...................................36
Hope..39

SEEKING LIGHT IN THE DARKNESS

The Stars In All Their Mystery..........................42
The Tempests Of Life...44
Estral..47
Heal The Hearts...49
Nature Of Man...51

CONTENTS

Angels Walk Among Us.................................53
Darkness..56
The Child Song...58
Until The End Of Days................................60
Screaming In The Darkness.........................63
Can Holy Men Past The Tests 65
The Battle Rages......................................67
Travelers In Time.....................................70

COMING HOME

Listen For God's Voice...............................74
In The Arms Of An Angel............................77
Listen To The Angels Sing..........................80
Journey Home 82
The Spirit To Receive 85
From The Mist The Angels Came...................88

Dedication

Time Of Angels Is At Hand

God sent a Heavenly Light into the darkness
Where no earthly light could fare
A Light to save His children
A Light to show God cares

And hope is on the horizon
For all who in darkness drown
For Heaven sent a King
Wearing a Holy Crown

He held the scales of justice
Mercy He did sound
This Holy King from Heaven
Wearing a Holy Crown

He stood before the darkness
He stands before this day
He holds a mirror of conscious
He is the Holy Way

He wears the Crown of Glory
The Lamb that Heaven sent
To fulfill the promises of Heaven
To teach us what was meant

When God in all His Glory
Told His children, who had gone
a stray
That He would send His Love
And show them a better Way

Amen Amen Amen

Angels Sing With Glory

Darkness could not contain Him
The Lamb that Heaven sent
The Son who with the Father
Took death from whom it was meant

The Angels sing with Glory
As God's army strikes its fear
In the demons in the night
As God holds His children near

The King that entered this world
Is the whisper that God sent
To cleanse this world of darkness
And take death from whom it was meant

The Angels sing with Glory
As God's army strikes its fear
In the demons in the night
As God holds His children near

And the whisper that was Heaven sent
Showed us with His life
That faith in God and forgiveness
Are stronger than any strife

The Angels sing with Glory
As God's army strikes its fear
In the demons in the night
As God holds His children near

As this whisper grew to a roar
Miracles behold
The Son of God was sent
As the prophets had foretold

The Angels sing with Glory
As God's army strikes its fear
In the demons in the night
As God holds His children near

To stand before the darkness
And say 'you have no hold'
On the children of the Father
The Shepherd protects His fold

Amen Amen Amen

Holding Hands With Jesus

Holding hands with Jesus
To the Promised Land
The Son of God will lead us
Every woman, child and man

When we are bent and broken
From the weight this life does bear
When pain and loss have shaken
And it is only misery we share

When promises are broken
And trust and honor have fallen
Because our faith was in mankind
When to Heaven we should be calling

When the faces of the tortured
Are seen most every day
We should raise our voice to Heaven
To find a better Way

Holding hands with Jesus
To the Promised Land
The Son of God will lead us
Every woman, child and man

When life has no forward movement
Because we are paralyzed by guilt and
fear
When we want freedom from
the darkness
We should call the Heavens near

When it seems that our spirits have left us
We are the walking dead
We should pray for hope and mercy
And remember what Jesus said

That our Father is always with us
As the shepherd with the sheep
That He sent His Son to save us
And His promises to keep

Holding hands with Jesus
To the Promised Land
The Son of God will lead us
Every woman, child and man

Amen Amen Amen

A Love Song

We should be singing love songs
As we give thanks and praise
For the promises of Heaven
For our blessings every day

We should be singing love songs
For the Angels Heaven sent
For the wonder of life
For love as it was meant

We should be singing love songs
To God as we were told
That He sent us a Love Song
A Miracle to behold

A Song of Love and Mercy
Of courage with no bounds
A Song of justice and compassion
A Song that through eternity sounds

And as this Song fills our worlds
And frees us from our strife
A Song of understanding
A Song of eternal life

A Song that fills the Heavens
And Angels sing with Love
The Son of God was sent
A Love Song from above

Amen Amen Amen

Divinity

Holiness in its splendor
Father, Spirit and the Son
God in all His Glory
Holiness Three in One

Flame eternal
Dove, Lion and Lamb
The mysteries of Heaven
The Great I Am

The Voice and the conscious
The heart and the cross
The sacrifice for man
Dark ways were lost

The tree of life
The sacraments abound
The Holiness of Heaven
The mysteries that surround

The Spirit of the Father
The Father and the Son
The Angels sent from Heaven
The Holy Three in One

Amen Amen Amen

Faith

As the dark armies advance
Terror and chaos are everywhere
The legions of the Light
Will bring Holiness to bear

As darkness seems to over take these worlds
And mankind is filled with horror and grief
To stand against the darkness
One must have his belief

That faith in God will carry
That faith in God will soar
That faith in God will break the bonds
And destroy the dark army's roar

That Light dissolves the darkness
That night turns into day
That praying to the Lord
To make a better Way

Will be answered with His Angels
Will be answered Heaven sent
Will be answered by the Voice of God
Will show us what was meant

When the Shepherd stands before His fold
When the Father protects the Son
When Angels stand before darkness
And the souls of men are won

Amen Amen Amen

Living Flames Of Heaven

The lights that brighten this world
Are often Heaven sent
To guide us through our darkness
As only God has meant

These lights are blessings
That are sent from above
Regardless of their forms
They are sent with God's true Love

A Love that has no boundaries
A Love that can not be contained
In the frailties of these worlds
To save us from our pain

The Living Flames of Heaven
Can take on any guise
Open up your hearts
And God's signs you will recognize

See the uniqueness of creation
See the hearts behind the masks
See the Holiness of life
To care is not a task

God can speak in whispers
God can speak in roars
Holiness abounds us
Love and Mercy soars

Hold the hand that is offered
Wipe away the tears
Love the ones discarded
Dissolve the darkest fears

The lights that brighten this world
Are often Heaven sent
To guide us through the darkness
As only God has meant

Amen Amen Amen

Jesus Is The Song

Jesus is the Song of Heaven
What is the song of man
Does our music reflect our cultures
Does it fill us with the hope to expand

The boundaries of this existence
The limits of time and space
Or is it filled with darkness
And scream with hatred and rage

What songs do we teach our children
to sing
What words fill their hearts
The Song of Heaven
Or a world that is dark

We sought to expand our boundaries
But within the world of man
Jesus help us to transcend these vessels
Jesus grasp our unholy hands

Let us sing songs of freedom
That hope and love may fill our worlds
Let the voices of the Heavens
Teach us the Angel's Holy words

Let our songs stand up to darkness
Let our songs bring forth the Light
Let our songs ask for forgiveness
Let our songs disempower the night

Lord teach us the Words of Heaven
Let Your Holiness pour forth
Let creation sing with Angels
Let the songs for evermore

Break the chains that bind us
Help us to understand
That Jesus will save us
Every woman, child and man

Amen Amen Amen

Wonderment

The wonder of His Glory
The wonder of His feats
The wonder of His Holiness
He defeated the great beasts

The world will gaze with wonder
As darkness turns to day
As hordes of satan's armies
Are driven from their prey

The worlds will fill with wonder
As the Song of Heaven rings
When the Angels gather for us
Their Heavenly voices to sing

The Song that fills the Heavens
The Song of God Himself
The Song that rings through the ages
To deliver us from hell

Amen Amen Amen

Abundance

Let the wings of Angels surround you
Let God hold you in His Hands
Let the blessings of Heaven abound for you
Let God's children return to the Holy land

May you always have Light in the darkness
May you hear the Voice of God
May you see with the heart of an Angel
May you walk where no man has trod

Amen Amen Amen

Bless Us With Your Presence

Let God, of all the worlds that ever were
And all the worlds that ever will be
Of all times, of all ages, of all creation...

Bless us with Your Presence
Consume us with Your Grace
Walk with us
In the darkness of this place

Surround us with Your Angels
Carry us on Your Wings
Give us the Voice of Heaven
Your Holiness to sing

Give us the faith of Angels
The strength and courage of Your
Holy kings
Let our voices never falter
Let the words of Heaven ring

Never let the Flames be stilled
Nor darkness stop the dance
Let the power of the Holy Spirit
Teach the Holy chants

Let Jesus walk among us
And teach us how to open the door
To transcend the chains that bind us
To allow our spirits to soar

Amen Amen Amen

A Little Angel

A little Angel was sent to earth
To prepare the Holy Way
To open the hearts of people
For the most glorious of days

This little Angel taught God's children
Who had forgotten the Holy Ways
That the Lord is always with us
Until the end of days

She sang the Songs of Heaven
She brought the Spirit in
To the most forgotten creatures
To help redeem them from their sin

She sang the praises
Of the most ancient of Kings
And she reminded the world of Angels
The Holy Songs did ring

A path she lit in the darkness
The words she taught of the Song
She blessed a world of darkness
And asked God to heal the wrongs

The Angel, she created
Lights to show the Way
So sheep could find the Shepherd
Until night turned into day

Amen Amen Amen

The White Bird Of Christmas

The white bird of Heaven
Came down from above
God sent a messenger
To carry a message of Love

Free and inspired
He flew and he flew
To carry God's message
To everyone who

Would listen to the Spirit
Would let their hearts be filled with
Love
Wanted forgiveness
And redemption from above

This white bird from Heaven
Gave off a Holy Light
So all God's children
Could find Him in the night

The white bird from Heaven
He sang and he sang
He reminded the people
From where they began

Amen Amen Amen

Blood And The Crown

The baby wrapped in swaddling
That shivered in the cold
Was the Heavenly King sent to us
As the prophets had foretold

Honored by the wise men
Regal gifts they bestowed
Rubies, gold and spices
Miracles behold

Shepherds knelt before Him
Awed by Holiness and Grace
How blessed were these beings
To see God's Holy Face

The Song of creation
Was realized that night
As God blessed a dark world
With Holiness and Light

As He ministered to the needy
As He taught us to pray
He freed our spirits
And showed us a better Way

To understand the living
To conquer the dead
To believe in the Eternal Father
For 'we are God's children', He said

He taught us with His actions
He taught us with His words
He cleansed us with His Presence
His Holy Voice was heard

In all the worlds below us
In all the worlds above
He conquered the darkest regions
He blessed us with God's Love

Blood and the crown
Redemption is found
Forgiveness and faith
Blessed with Holy Grace

Amen Amen Amen

Hope

A cry came from the darkness
A voice so sweet and pure
The crying of an infant
To bring the Heavens near

As He lay before them
They were filled with Holy Grace
The men from every nation
Every creed and every race

From such humble beginnings
Came this Gift of Love
To save us from the nightmares
To bless us from above

The Course that He would show us
The path that He would take
Was Heaven's way of teaching
That God would not forsake

The children He gave life to
The children that He loves
He sent His Son to save us
To Bless us from above

A cry came from the darkness
A voice so sweet and pure
That conquered death's dark power
To bring the Heavens near

Amen Amen Amen

Seeking Light In The Darkness

The Stars In All Their Mystery

As I look into the darkness
I can not believe my eyes
There is radiance and luster
Illuminating in the skies

The stars in all their mystery
Are dancing with Holy glee
For on this Christmas night
A world is paying tribute to Thee

Was it only yesterday
Or thousands of years since Thee
Sent Your Light to guide us
Your Son to set us free

I am filled with wonder
As I look at this Christmas sky
At the lights that brighten this world
At a Love that cannot die

A Light showed man the path to
Heaven
And thousands of years since
The Christmas lights still illuminate
There are no coincidences

God thank You for sending
Your Holy Light into our dark worlds

Amen Amen Amen

The Tempests Of Life

The tempests of life seek to distract us
From the Holy tests we live
The nature of mankind attacks us
Your Love we pray You give

Our dreams turn into nightmares
Our perceptions to the test
Our hearts and faith are challenged
Until our time to rest

Lord help us to understand our journeys
Lord help us to know why we have this life
Lord carry us through these tests
Lord save us from man's rife

Of darkness, pain and sorrow
Of hatred, power and greed
Of our need to commit horror
Of the darkness of our deeds

Help us to understand that
These tests are seen by Thee
Our thoughts, our words our actions
Are known to the power of Three

Nothing is hidden from Heaven
No matter how hard man tries
God knows the motivations
The sacrifices and the lies

Lord, give us understanding
To overcome the challenges and strife
Send us Your Holy Blessings
And walk with us on this path of life

Amen Amen Amen

Estral

Lord my heart would pray to Heaven
To shelter us through this path of life
To awaken the Holiness within us
To teach us how to overcome our strife

To explain this Holy journey
To guide us through the night
To send us stars from Heaven
Our pathways to make bright

To give us the courage to be warriors
The hearts of Angels as foretold
The faith of the Heavens
To never let our souls be sold

As one voice cries from the darkness
As one voice asks of the power of
Three
To conquer this world of chaos
To teach Your children of the Love of
Thee

Amen Amen Amen

Heal The Hearts

The heart of a mother
Weeps with the pain
Of a child that she lost
Of a life to regain

The insanity that surrounds us
Is hard to explain
When a life is lost
And nothing is gained

Despair has no equal
Sorrow, a burden to bear
Questions unanswered
Grief unable to share

God bless the mothers
The hearts filled with pain
The lost and the crippled
The sacrificed to the insane

Bless them with comfort
And release them from pain
The Spirit of God
His healing to gain

Bless all Your children
In this world filled with strife
Bless them with Love
And Your Holy Light

Amen Amen Amen

Nature Of Man

Is suicide the nature of mankind
We conquer a people to take their land
We destroy their spirits
A dark tribute to man

The land, too, is a victim
Of power and greed
We ravish and plunder
And take more than we need

We destroy all the animals
The bees and the birds
The wonder of life
May no longer be heard

God speaks in whispers
No life is inane
Except in a world
Destroyed by the insane

We poison our life force
Our water and air
The world is dying
Take notice and care

God deliver us from this madness
And the darkness we wed
So our children will not inherit
A world of the dead

Amen Amen Amen

Angels Walk Among Us

Angels walk among us
Save us from disgrace
Protect us from our choices
Your Holy Light to replace

The darkness that defeats us
The sin that weighs us down
The fear and guilt and horror
That would block us from Your Crown

Angels walk among us
And heal us with Your Love
May Your Holy Presence
Bring blessings from above

Angels walk among us
And show us as You see
Break the chains that bind us
And set God's children free

Angels walk among us
In these unholy battle grounds
Save us from the terror
And fill us with the sound

Of the Holiness of Heaven
Of the Song the Angels sing
Of the Voice of our Lord
His Holy words to bring

Us to the Holy places
The paths we had once tread
We will remember sacred faces
We will no longer walk among the dead

Amen Amen Amen

Darkness

A cloud of darkness covers
The world of man as known
A cloud of fear and oppression
A darkness man condones

We call this cloud upon us
This cloud of terror and greed
We wed the darkness in it
To satisfy our needs

This dark cloud feeds our demons
And multiplies in size
By the anguish and the fear
By the victims painful cries

We have seen this dark cloud
approaching
We have seen its evil face
Why does no one call to the Heavens
To save us with God's Grace

God stand before the darkness
Destroy the demons within
Save us from this madness
Cleanse us from our sin

Amen Amen Amen

The Child Song

A child in the night
His eyes wide with fear
God, bless him and keep him
And always hold him near

To the heart of an Angel
To the Shepherd and King
To the Son from above
Of whom Angels sing

Come little children
Be not afraid
For the Lord will stand before you
Your ransom is paid

Come little children
A star to behold
The Lord God will bless you
As scriptures foretold

And unto Jesus
This child of the night
Will know the Love of Heaven
Will be in God's Holy Sight

Amen Amen Amen

Until The End Of Days

When darkness over takes me
And in the chaos I go astray
When I am blind and I am injured
And to my death I lay

I will call upon You, Lord
And ask to be shown the Way
And I will sing You love songs
Until the end of days

When I stumble and I fall
From the burdens of this life
When I lose myself in the darkness
When I am filled with strife

I will call upon You, Lord
And ask to be shown the Way
And I will sing You love songs
Until the end of days

When weary from the torment
And the hatred that I wear
When this world of chaos
Is more than I can bear

I will call upon You, Lord
And ask to be shown the Way
And I will sing You love songs
Until the end of days

When my breath is fading
And my body yearns to sleep
When the frailties of this life
My strength no longer keeps

I will call unto You, Lord
And ask to be shown the Way
And I will sing You love songs
Until the end of days

When my heart stops beating
And my spirit is set free
When my God comes for me
And I will truly see

I will sing You love songs
Until the end of days

Amen Amen Amen

Screaming In The Darkness

Men raise their voices in anguish
To be heard above the din
They are sinking in the darkness
They are crippled from within

Louder and louder are the voices
As terror within them rise
As the fragile vessels fail
As they lose their human guise

They are screaming in the darkness
They are searching for their own voice
They are terrified by their surroundings
They have created, by their own choice

God send Your Light from Heaven
To show us our Way Home
Send us Your Grace and Forgiveness
With You we are never alone

Save us from the hells we have created
Fill us with Your Love
Let terror no longer rule us
Return us to our Home above

Amen Amen Amen

Can Holy Men Past The Tests

There are those who would represent holiness
But darkness masks their treason
They deny and betray
Greed and power are the reasons

They wear the mask of God
And freely utter His word
Yet, they victimize His flocks
The voice of darkness is all they have heard

What a gain it is for darkness
God's children to betray
To defile the Holy dwellings
To cause innocents to stray

When the men of holiness
Are too weak to past the tests
They glorify the body
Not the Spirit of the blessed

God save us from the demons
Who holy masks would display
Expose the darkness in them
Save Your children from going astray

Amen Amen Amen

The Battle Rages

The battle rages
A warrior dies
God welcomes him
He transcends the skies

What song do they march to
To whom do they serve
What allegiance do they honor
What honors do they deserve

The warriors of heroes
The warriors of men
The warriors of Heaven
All time to transcend

The tear of an Angel
As Holiness weeps
For the pain of mankind
The blood runs deep

The wounds of the warrior
How deep do they heal
The horror of war
Man's soul does it steal

God's Holy armies
Soar from above
To conquer the darkness
To heal with God's love

God protect Your children
From terror and hate
From the fortress of hell
From the unholy gate

God protect creation
From tyranny and greed
From the nature of man
From their unholy deeds

Amen Amen Amen

Travelers In Time

As we travel through the dark night
Our Savior to behold
As the shepherds and the wise men
As the Angels foretold

Lights from Heaven will guide us
As they did, the men of old
For God is always with us
As the prophets foretold

The night is thick with darkness
Our bodies ravaged and cold
Fear may overtake us
Some may lose their souls

But the journey that we travel
Tests us by our choices
Do we pray upon our knees
Do we raise our holy voices

Or do we hide in the darkness
To cloak our sinful deeds
Do we call upon the demons
To feed our unholy needs

As we travel through the dark night
With many paths to choose
Do we follow the Heavenly Lights
Do we chance our souls to lose

God, may You always walk with us
May You send a Light to guide
May You shelter and protect us
May Your Holy Presence abide

God may we stay on the path
The Course of which Miracles are made
May the travelers in time
Turn their nights into days

Amen Amen Amen

Coming Home

Listen For God's Voice

Because we do not recognize God's Voice
Does not mean He is not speaking
We overlook His Holy signs
Because they are not in the forms we are seeking

We let our vision narrow
We do not allow ourselves to see
That there may be more to life
Than what is in front of you and me

We dismiss the Songs He sings us
We ignore what He has sent
We do not seek to know
The journey as it was meant

We build our walls around us
With darkness and with fear
We blind our own eyes
We cover our ears

We say that He has forsaken
And left us on this dark way
We get angry
And refuse to pray

God is always near us
Though we fail to see
The blessings that He has sent
May be in a different form than we

Had asked that He would give us
Had asked to make a priority
Because there may be more to life
Than what is in front of you and me

Open up your hearts and souls
And let God's Presence in
Listen for His Voice
And you will hear it in the din

Amen Amen Amen

In The Arms Of An Angel

The tears of a father
Who buries a son
Questions the Heavens
For a life yet begun

Overwhelmed with anguish
Overcome with grief
There is no answer, no reason
Which can give him relief

How does a shepherd
Morn the loss of a sheep
The father, protector
His promise to keep

When life has lost meaning
And we walk with the dead
Remember the scriptures
The words, Jesus said

God is the Father
His children to keep
Heavenly Home
No longer to weep

Wings of an Angel
Arms of the Lord
Transcends all ages
Spirits to soar

Peace without anguish
Life without pain
Reunited with the Father
Together again

Amen Amen Amen

Listen To The Angels Sing

We listen to the Angels sing
A Song so sweet and pure
A Song that transcends ages
A Song we long to hear

Wings of gold will carry
The messengers with their Song
The music will inspire
The message will correct what is wrong

As we listen to their voices
Would we worlds transcend
On the wings of Holy messengers
Our lives will have no end

As we listen to their voices
Overwhelmed and filled with tears
As our hearts are opened
And the Song brings Heaven near

Amen Amen Amen

Journey Home

A journey long has started
A quest to find our way
To a Home we have forgotten
To find a better Way

A journey of the ancients
A passage of the tests
Awaken from the nightmares
Is the Holy quest

The road is long and arduous
With obstacles that may hide
The path that we are seeking
God, with us abide

We can not make this journey
Without God at our side
Give us what we need
God, with us abide

A Light within the darkness
A shelter in the storm
A Savior to protect us
As the demons swarm

There are so many obstacles
If we lose our way
Pray that God will carry
And make a better Way

To make this Holy journey
We must ask to hear
God's Voice in the darkness
To bring the Heavens near

Amen Amen Amen

The Spirit To Receive

The Angel stood before me
My eyes I thought deceived
Then a voice rang through me
And the Spirit to receive

'You pray for all God's children'
'That darkness may not deceive'
'That God will bless and keep them'
And the Spirit to receive

'And every prayer has merit'
'The prayers of those who believe'
'Are answered by the Heavens'
The Spirit to receive

'We answer those who call to us'
'We answer those who pray'
'But people get discouraged'
'Because they do not understand the Holy Way'

'Faith is more than presents'
'More than you can see with your eyes'
'Learn to see with your heart'
'And you will see through the disguise'

'That this world would have you believe in'
'That this world would have you fear'
'Simply raise your voice to Heaven'
'And bring the Angels near'

'The darkness can be conquered'
'A world of hate to leave'
'Simply raise your voice to Heaven'
The Spirit to receive

Amen Amen Amen

From The Mist
The Angels Came

From the mist
The Angels came
To save creation
In Heaven's name

The King of Angels
The ancient Lord
Came with blessings
The dove and the sword

And all creation
Bows before
The King of Kings
The Angels soar

The Lamb, the Lion
The dove and the sword
Forgives His children
And creation soars

The King of Kings
The Angels sing

Amen Amen Amen

God In All His Glory
Told His Children,
Who Had Gone A Stray
That He Would Send His Love
And Show Them A Better Way
Amen
Amen
Amen

www.ingramcontent.com/pod-product-compliance
Lightning Source LLC
Chambersburg PA
CBHW051709040426
42446CB00008B/792